I0037428

FIVE
Steps

A Proven Formula for Launching
a Successful Healthcare
Staffing Agency

Nicole Caillier, Ph.D.

FIVE STEPS

A Proven Formula for Launching a Successful Healthcare Staffing Agency

By Nicole Caillier, Ph.D.

© 2023 Quality Staffing Network LLC.

All rights reserved. No part of this publication may be reproduced, distributed, or transmitted in any form or by any means, including photocopying, recording, or other electronic or mechanical methods, without the prior written permission of the copyright holder, except in the case of brief quotations embodied in critical reviews and certain other noncommercial uses permitted by copyright law.

Book Design by Transcendent Publishing | www.transcendentpublishing.com

ISBN: 979-8-9885147-8-7

The Author has strived in every way to be as accurate and complete as possible in the creation of this book, notwithstanding the fact that she does not warrant or represent at any time that the contents within the book are accurate due to the rapidly changing nature of the subject.

While all attempts have been made to verify each and every piece of information provided in this publication, the Author assumes no responsibility for any errors, omissions, or contrary interpretation of the subject matter herein.

The author makes no guarantees concerning the level of success you may experience by following the advice and strategies contained in this book, and you accept the risk that results will differ for each individual. The testimonials and examples provided in this book show exceptional results, which may not apply to the average reader, and are not intended to represent or guarantee that you will achieve the same or similar results.

Dedication

To my husband, you have shown me a love that knows no limits. I cherish your unwavering belief in me and my dreams. Your support has given me the strength to embrace any and every season. Thank you for constantly reminding me − I am not alone!

To my son, who gave me the courage, inspiration, and a reason to pursue my dreams to the fullest. I am forever grateful.

To my daughters, my precious angels, you inspire me to be the best version of myself. I am forever grateful for the incredible bond that we share and the way you embrace me as I am. Thank you for the love, laughter, and purpose that you've brought into my world.

Contents

Introduction

*Sometimes good things fall apart
so a better thing can fall together.*

–Marilyn Monroe

Back in 2005, I was twenty-six years old and working as a nurse. Life was good. I enjoyed my work and excelled at it; my coworkers consistently complimenting me on having the latest Crocs and always being "put together." However, while I was passionate about caring for and being of service to others, I also knew that I ultimately wanted something more for myself.

I thought I was on my way to that "something" when I got a promotion – and not just because it meant a bump in salary. The new position, which was offered to me out of the blue when someone was out on medical leave, was on the corporate level generating revenue for the facility. In one day, I went from running around the facility doing the thousands of things nurses do each shift, and the next I was in an office, responsible for large sums of money. I didn't know what I was doing, but I figured, "I can handle this for two weeks." When the woman I was filling in for decided not to return, I was asked to take over permanently.

It was as if I had been transported into a new world. Not only would I be getting a bump in salary, I would be getting back more of my time. There would be no more weekends, no more bedside nursing. I was told, "Nicole, you're going to have freedom. You're going to have more control over your schedule. You're going to have flexibility."

This sounded amazing! I mean, I don't know anyone who doesn't want more flexibility, and as a mom, this was particularly important. I felt like my life was definitely on an upward trajectory.

After working hard and settling into my new position for a while, I went to talk to my supervisor about how I could start tapping into this culture of flexibility I had heard about. After what I thought was a great conversation, I headed back to my office feeling once again like I was on the precipice of an exciting new time in my career. I thought I had "made it."

I was still feeling pretty great about myself when she showed up at my door about fifty minutes later. At first I thought the paperwork in her hand had to do with my new "flexibility," but then I noticed something about her demeanor was different...something had happened. Before I could say anything, she walked up to me, handed me the papers, and said, "Nicole, you're fired."

You know when you're so shocked you feel frozen in place? Well, that's how I felt. I wasn't moving, wasn't speaking, but in my head I was thinking, *Girl, you can't fire me! I just got a raise. I just got a promotion. How can this be happening?!*

A few minutes later, I was being marched past my co-workers and out of the building like a criminal. My humiliation in that moment was matched only by my confusion. For the life of me, I still didn't know what had brought on this devasting event. It was like I had been the victim of a hit-and-run.

As I stood in the parking lot my thoughts ran to my son, of whom I was the primary caregiver. The reason I was fired didn't matter, I realized. I had to figure out what I was going to do to provide for him, and quick.

First things first, though: I was going to go across the street (where no one from work would see me) and have a good cry. And cry I did – one of those uncontrollable, ugly cries that you really want to be alone for. As I sobbed, it dawned on me that beneath the humiliation and the anger at my supervisor, I was also directing quite a bit of anger at myself. For the first time I realized that I had put someone else in control of my time, my income, and my freedom. I had put myself in a position where the rug could be pulled out from underneath me, without warning, at any moment.

Though I didn't know it at the time, that realization would be a turning point in my life. It was the moment I decided to never be in that position again.

For some time I had been thinking about starting my

own business. In my ideal scenario, when I did it I would have a full-time, dependable job and a safety net in the bank, allowing me to feel comfortable as I worked on the business in my spare time. But life and God had another plan, one that required an accelerated timetable and a willingness to deal with a whole lot of *disc*omfort.

After doing some research, I decided to start a business helping other nurses find jobs. I was well aware of how crazy this sounded, considering I had just been fired from my own nursing job, but the idea took hold and wouldn't let go. And it worked! Of course, my journey has been a little more complicated than that, and there have been plenty of bumps along the way. We'll touch on those points throughout the book. My point is that though I was shocked, humiliated, and angry that day, I still took action and, no matter where you are in life, so can you.

I freely admit that in the early days of my business I had no clue what I was doing; I just started making phone calls. I called facilities I used to work for. I called former colleagues I had worked alongside. I reached out to everyone I could think of in the healthcare field, knowing that I was offering a valuable service and that each call was a step toward getting my staffing agency off the ground.

My efforts paid off, and within that first year, I had several clients. Ironically, one of the largest was the facility that had fired me, to the tune of a quarter of a million dollars — a satisfying twist, if I ever saw one! By the second-year mark, I was well on my way to building the company to six figures… And then, just when things were getting really exciting, it all fell apart.

Suddenly, I found myself working as a janitor for my husband's business. Now, there's nothing wrong with being a janitor, but it was a far cry from running a successful healthcare staffing firm.

Again, I found myself asking, "What happened?"

Well, for one, it wasn't actually "sudden." Remember, when I started out I didn't know what I was doing – *I just did it.* And for those two years I'd tried to figure everything out, working with the knowledge I had and thinking that any problems would fix themselves. People kept telling me, "Get insight, get information, get a coach," but I didn't want to hear it. I was determined to do it all on my own.

I didn't realize that I was building a house on sand.

My wake-up call came while I was scrubbing those toilets and vacuuming floors, thinking, *What in the world am I doing here?* It was another one of those pivotal moments when a major shift in awareness leads to major life changes. What followed is what I like to call my "Ph.D. education" in staffing. I stopped learning about staffing and I started learning about business. I started learning about leadership. I started challenging myself.

In both cases – when I was fired and when I had to rebuild my business – starting over, turned out to be "the better thing" Marilyn Monroe talked about. It forced me to go back to the basics, acquire the knowledge and the assistance I needed, and learn to construct my house on a solid foundation. A critical piece of this was engaging my first mentor, a woman I still credit with helping me get where I am today. This is why I talk so much about the value of mentorship and why I have invested so heavily in it throughout my journey.

In the seventeen years since I left that nursing job, I've employed thousands of people, created countless solutions, and generated millions in revenue. I have also launched nearly four hundred healthcare staffing firms, some of which are also multimillion-dollar enterprises. Most importantly, however, I have reclaimed my time and my income – and realized my mission of empowering others to do the same thing.

To this end, I've curated some of the best lessons from healthcare staffing I have learned over the years. The result is a proprietary framework that teaches you how to launch your own firm in four phases: legal, administrative, operational, and executive.

This book is for you if:

- You want to start a healthcare staffing firm but don't know where to start.

- You're ready to stop trading dollars for hours and own your time.

- You want to accelerate your success in the healthcare staffing industry and need guidance and clarity on how to begin.

- You have already started a healthcare staffing firm and are ready to take it to the next level.

- You have another type of business and want to add healthcare staffing as a profit center.

- You are ready to dream big, bring your A-game, and go all in to make this happen.

That said, there are a few other things you should know about me before we begin – the first being that I am a woman of faith and conviction. I believe that I was called by God to do the work I do, and the successes I have realized in my life (as well as the formula for success I offer others) started out as prayers. Therefore, when teaching I speak often about God and the importance of asking for what we want. I also talk about money *a lot* – what it really is and what it can do for us – and how we need to get really specific about much we need to generate in order to create the lives we desire. My platform is about *transformation* and *wealth* – healthcare staffing is merely a vehicle for that. So if money and God are uncomfortable topics, you might *really* be thrown to hear that I talk about how the two relate to each other! Finally, I am a woman of both great confidence and great humility. I know what I know, and I also understand the value of being a lifelong learner. When I am the student, I set aside any preconceived notions I have and show up ready to listen with an open mind. When I am the teacher, it is "my house," and I expect those who enter to do the same. For example, when I challenge your beliefs about money – both philosophically (i.e., that money is "bad" or that material wealth and spirituality are mutually exclusive) and practically (i.e., the way you make financial decisions), approach what I'm saying with openness, a willingness to learn, and respect for the knowledge and experience I have acquired throughout my journey.

If this resonates with you, keep reading. The chapters that follow correspond to my five steps for creating massive income and impact in the billion-dollar healthcare staffing industry. I teach you how to keep your costs low and your profits high, why all staffing niches are not equal, and how to weather the inevitable storms that arise. Even more important than processes, procedures, and action steps, you will learn about how to step into an identity of abundance, not just in dollars and sense, but in terms of time, balance, and freedom. You will also meet several of our exemplary mentees, some of whom may have started out with fewer resources and more challenges than you, whose firms are not only building real, sustainable wealth for themselves and their families, but making it possible for them to positively impact communities and, by extension, the world.

Are you ready? Now let's begin!

Chapter One

GO FAST (WEALTH HAS A NEED FOR SPEED)

A mentor once told me, "Whoever goes first gets more." When you wait to start your business, you are missing out on a piece of the pie. In this chapter I'm going to give you a formula that empowers you to begin making decisions for your healthcare staffing firm *today*. More importantly, I'm going to explain some of the mental traps we fall into and how to cultivate the right mindset, because without that all the formulas in the world won't help.

You can learn a great deal about mental fortitude from watching the show *My 600-Lb Life*. It follows the journey of several individuals who are given a strict weight loss program, and often gastric bypass surgery, so they can get healthy and create the lives they want. What moves me is the emotional process they go through as they excavate and untangle the real reasons they became obese in the first place. Each person has a unique story, but the message is the same: their success hinges upon, not just what is on their plate, but what's happening in their minds. These brave individuals are living proof that it doesn't matter where you start your journey, but where you finish.

Here are some common mental hurdles I have seen (and personally experienced) from people wanting to start their own healthcare staffing firm, and ways to overcome them.

- **A Misstated Mission.** If you're in the healthcare field, you are likely drawn to being of service. This is a noble and admirable purpose – one that I share. However, when I hear someone saying that they *just* want to serve, the alarm bells go off. My first two years in business, everything was fueled by passion – "I love it. It's going to be wonderful. I'm a nurse. I love it. I want to help nurses. I want to help facilities." I said this right up to the moment I found myself at zero, with no facilities and no employees, but having learned a valuable lesson about the importance of profitability. You can have all the purpose, passion, excitement, and zeal in the world, but without revenue it goes nowhere. If this is the space you're in, it's time to investigate what's going on beneath the surface; for example, beliefs that money is the root of all evil or that you can't love what you do and be financially abundant.

- **Mixing Business and Therapy.** Another barrier to success is treating your company as a source of self-worth, which can lead to overattachment to every outcome and analysis paralysis when making decisions. In fact, most people have no idea about the value of their own services, and they act from this space when meeting with potential clients and even interacting with their employees.

As we will discuss throughout this book, a business built on emotion is one built on sand and eventually will crumble. The fix: do the development work needed to go from employee to CEO. This can be counseling, coaching, or whatever it takes for you to go from a "Will you please work with me," or punching-the-clock mentality to recognizing that you are the solution to your client's problem. It also means drawing strong boundaries and not taking things, be it criticism or a "no," personally. Remember, all work is profitable – the question is whether it is going to profit you, or someone else. Most entrepreneurs quit because someone told them no when really they just need to pivot.

> o Mentee tip: Don't be afraid to go back to clients and ask the right questions to make things mutually beneficial, even if means re-engaging and renegotiating an untenable contract. If you enter into an agreement that's not profitable, you're working for nothing.

- **Being Sloppy with Their Vibe.** Where is your energy level? I am at ten all day, and I look to speak with people who are at a twelve. This is critical to shifting your mindset, and your identity. For example, start telling yourself, "I have something in common with the most successful people out there." Let it settle in your bones. Own it, for it is more important than any activity and strategy.

- **Closed Ears, Closed Mind.** Stepping outside your comfort zone means learning, and sometimes that means hearing uncomfortable truths. Be discerning about who you listen to, and when they point out what you're doing or not doing to build success, pay attention.

It's likely you recognized at least one of these patterns within yourself; in fact, if you didn't I would encourage you to go back and take a closer look. We all have less-than-productive habits; what sets us apart is how we shift them. If this sounds daunting, consider these words from Henry Ford: "Nothing is particularly hard if you divide it into small jobs." The participants on *My 600-Lb Life* are facing an incredibly difficult challenge, one that may seem complicated – maybe even impossible. Then they get a roadmap, a way to move toward their goal one pound, one workout, one meal at a time. Along the way, they will also be working out some of the thoughts and attitudes that have held them back in the past. It is the same with any endeavor, including launching and running your healthcare staffing business. Your mindset will change when you transform, when you get access to information that makes you reevaluate everything you were thinking before. That's the real work, and success comes when you are able to say to yourself, "Wow, I was thinking small!" It is my job, my mission, to provide you with the strategy to get there, one step at a time.

Now, let's get into the money.

What's Your Number? (Determining Your Year-One Revenue)

The first step to getting what you want is knowing what you want, writing the vision, and making it plain. The first step in creating that vision is setting the amount you want to make your first year in healthcare staffing.

Don't make this hard. You just need a number. What is your financial goal? If your first reaction is to say you don't have one, take a moment to reconsider. This is not just about figuring out what you need to make your rent, mortgage, or car payment each month; it's that magical number that pops into your head whenever you think about the business and the lifestyle you dream about. You may not have articulated it, but that's exactly what I am asking you to do now, because it is a foundational part of the process.

This number is going to be your barometer for growth. It will also help you solidify your geography and strategize for client acquisition and the onboarding of staff.

Is it fifty thousand dollars? How about seventy-five?

Before you answer, I want to clarify something: we're not here to make ten, fifteen, twenty, or even a hundred thousand dollars. Please do not take this as arrogance. I am simply very clear about the industry and who we attract. I regularly work with people who set million-dollar goals. Again, this is not shade or pie-in-the-sky thinking. It is what's possible working with a solid revenue formula. Now, think about your number again. Perhaps, given what I just said, that fifty- or seventy-five-thousand-dollar goal no longer looks as good as it did a minute ago!

It may not be a million dollars; it might be five hundred or seventy-five thousand. It might be two million. The choice is yours, and it could and should change over time. Moreover, it will not be based on a false ceiling or misconceptions, but on your most ambitious goals backed up by a formula that has been proven to work time and time again.

Now, let's get to it. Once you've set your year-one revenue goal, it's time to determine your profit margin. For the sake of this experiment, we'll use sixteen dollars an hour. This means that if your goal is one million dollars, you're going to divide that by sixteen.

Various geographic regions will have different parameters – we'll get into that in the next chapter. For now, just note that when you divide a million by sixteen you get 62,500. That means you will need to fill 62,500 hours annually with registered nurses, certified nursing assistants (CNAs), and medical assistants.

Next, divide that by twelve, for the number of months in a year – or 5,208 hours per month. There are four weeks in a month, so divide the monthly figure by four – or 1,302 hours per week. You will then divide that number by the shift – either eight or twelve, depending on what your facilities' preferences are. If we're talking about eight-hour shifts, you will need to fill 162 shifts per week to achieve your million-dollar goal.

But we're not done...

We also need to know how many people must be at work every day. Divide the number of shifts by seven and you will need a minimum of 23. Now you have a roundabout figure to use in your client acquisition plan. Do you see how even a goal as large as a million dollars can be broken down into something manageable?

One of the great things about healthcare staffing is that once you bring on a client, it's usually an ongoing relationship. That said, you're likely going to have a mix of large and small clients, especially in the beginning. A large client is one that has consistent staffing needs – usually anywhere from seven to twenty shifts per day – and you're handling that schedule for them pretty much around the clock. Smaller clients may have a shift here and there, or perhaps their needs ebb and flow and are not as dependable. If you're wondering (stressing about) the number of clients you will have or how to land those large clients, we'll get to that. For now, just keep in mind that when I made my first million dollars, I had just *four* clients.

Your Launch Date

This is another step that sometimes brings out a strong reaction in people. It presents an instant time crunch, and therefore pressure. *How can I pick a date when I don't know X, Y, and Z yet?* Stop and take a breath. *You* don't need to have everything figured out at this point. You just need to pick a date that we will use to *reverse-engineer* your staffing firm.

The only criterion is that you choose a launch date within six weeks of starting the process. This may sound like too short of a time, so you're going to have to trust me on this. Why? Because we have done it this way several hundred times.

Data-Driven Insights

We've looked at your revenue goal and setting your launch date. Next, we're going to check out the data. I generally don't answer random questions; I believe in strategy, and without the proper context I might not be giving you the information you need.

A pivotal moment for me was when my mentor said, "If you want to get the right answers, you've got to ask the right questions." We see evidence of this in our everyday lives, for example, when we have to tweak a Google search in order to get information relevant to our needs. Other times, it is much less obvious, yet the answers we receive are still being informed by the way we form the query. Recognizing this is a game-changer.

Many years ago, I was teaching my daughter Autumn, then age six, how to ride her bike. If you have ever taught a six-year-old how to ride a bike, then you already know this was drama.

We were all so excited that day as we rounded everybody up and went outside, ready to make an event of it. Her father padded her from the top of her head to the soles of her feet; there was no way our little girl was getting hurt!

"It's time, Autumn," we said, "Let's go."

As soon as we started walking down our driveway, Autumn's sense of adventure changed to fear. She started screaming, so loud some neighbors peeked out to see what was wrong.

Autumn turned to me andsaid, "Mama, Mama, what if I fall?"

In that moment, the light bulb went off.

Autumn was focused on the fall. She was focused on all the ways this first voyage wasn't going to work for her. She was focused on everything except what was in front of her. And because of that, she was asking me – and herself – the wrong question.

How many times have you been in this space? The space where you're askingyourself, "What if this doesn't work for me? What will I do if I fall (a.k.a. fail)?"

I looked back at Autumn and said, "What if you don't?"

As soon as the words left my mouth, I literally saw my daughter transform right before my eyes. Her expression went from, *"I don't know if I can do this"* to, *"I'm about to do this! I'm going to ride this bike!"*

A few seconds later, she was gliding triumphantly along the driveway.

The only thing that had changed was her focus. What would happen in your life if your focus changed? Can you imagine? Oftentimes, all you need to do so is to remind yourself to ask the right questions. And, speaking of which, I have added some here for you to consider.

Homework

What are your financial goals?

_____

_____

_____

_____

_____

_____

_____

_____

_____

_____

_____

_____

_____

_____

_____

_____

_____

_____

_____

_____

_____

_____

_____

_____

_____

_____

_____

Are you too emotionally attached (i.e., treating your business like therapy)?

_____

_____

_____

_____

_____

_____

_____

_____

_____

_____

_____

_____

_____

_____

_____

_____

_____

_____

_____

_____

_____

_____

_____

_____

_____

Do you know your worth?

_____

_____

_____

_____

_____

_____

_____

_____

_____

_____

_____

_____

_____

_____

_____

_____

_____

_____

_____

_____

_____

_____

_____

_____

_____

_____

_____

_____

What are your feelings about money?

_____
_____
_____
_____
_____
_____
_____
_____
_____
_____
_____
_____
_____
_____
_____
_____
_____
_____
_____
_____
_____
_____
_____
_____
_____
_____
_____

How do you approach prayer? Is it from a place of passivity (waiting for something to happen) or gratitude ("I know this is for meant for me")?

Chapter Two

FINDING YOUR SWEET SPOT (WHY GEOGRAPHY MATTERS)

uring my first attempt at running a healthcare staffing agency, from 2005 to 2007, I realized early success. I was making six figures, had tons of clients and a great reputation; I was fueled by a feeling of excitement that I was actually doing it. And that was the problem: I was operating on feelings. For example, I started in the region I live in, and only went to facilities where I had worked as a nurse and whose needs I was familiar with. I also assumed that people would come work for me for the same reason. In other words, I was making decisions from my comfort zone.

Well, I was in for a surprise. While some people did sign on, there were many others who were afraid of working for me, and rightfully so. I was twenty-six years old and a novice at running an agency. They were sticking to their own comfort zones as well!

Losing everything taught me several important lessons, the most valuable of which was the need to separate my emotions from data. When I relaunched, it was in a different, fertile geography.

We became national, and went from six figures to seven figures, in a relatively short amount of time. Again, we did this by looking solely looking at the data and moving to other regions that also supported expansion, and so on.

Take note of the difference between the two models. It wasn't the hard work I put in or my desire to achieve – that has always been one hundred and ten percent. The sole difference was that my first launch was based on feelings and emotions – what I thought, and what "they" said. The other was all about research. And that was the one that has been sustainable.

Now, I don't live a life of regrets, but I do reflect on the past and wonder how things could have played out differently. If I had used data to choose my geography from the start, I probably would have realized sustainable success earlier; I certainly wouldn't have had to work as a janitor until I got back on my feet. That experience, however, while painful, brought with it the revelation that wisdom and strategy, not guesswork and emotion, should be the foundation for every business decision.

It is natural to begin looking to launch in your own backyard. Starting your own business is stressful enough, you tell yourself, without trying to do it in an unfamiliar location. Take a minute to acknowledge this feeling, and then let it go. Remember, we are stepping into a new mindset, one that embraces growth and expansion, based on facts and figures. This means asking yourself, "Is there enough business in this area to support the growth of my agency?

Why is geography so important? To answer this question, I have to go back to revenue. Yes, I talk about money a lot, and about how to make six- and seven-figure revenues in the healthcare staffing industry. Why do I talk about it so much? Because others don't talk about it nearly enough. (If you are uncomfortable with that, re-read Chapter 1 and take the necessary steps to shift your money mindset). Also, we can't have a discussion about geography without discussing money, because that's where the money is. In fact, the "geography profit matrix" is key to any expansion plan for your business.

Scouting Locations

Now that you see the importance of approaching geography from a logical perspective rather than an emotional one, I'm going to go through a framework that will help you determine where you should launch.

Now, I am not saying that you cannot consider your immediate location. If there are vacancies there – great! The key is to use resources to determine whether the potential in the marketplace can support your revenue goal. Here's where having a solid plan for growth comes in. I see a lot of people with fragmented plans for growing their agencies because they're dead set on growing within a certain geography.

Staying in my local area would have been wonderful if my goal had continued to be five- to seven-hundred thousand dollars, because the market could support that. Once my goal crossed over into seven figures and beyond, everything changed.

What happened?

We expanded beyond our local geography and into new territories where there were different profit margins. There was also much more work available – in fact, the vacancies probably quadrupled. Remember the importance of asking the right questions? Well, instead of asking, "What are we proximal to?" we began to look at, "Where does the need exist in the market?"

Tapping Into Your Networks

I spoke with a nurse who really wanted to launch in a particular area. "I've been a nurse here for fifteen years," she told me. Sounds great, but I know the right questions to ask: "How many contacts do you have? How many facilities? How many administrators? How many directors of scheduling or whoever is in charge of the staffing process?"

She didn't have any.

I then asked, "How many nurses are you confident are going to sign on with you and work for your agency?"

She wasn't sure.

Do you see why we have to go back to the data and see if it makes sense to launch there? Let's say the data shows that the opportunity is better in another, unfamiliar location. She may "know" a lot of people in her home region, but if she does not have the connections to grow her business, I would advise her to roll the dice and launch in the new place. Again, take the emotion out of it.

Now, there are others I've spoken with who were in HR or nursing and know hundreds if not thousands of people and have a great reputation. Then it might make sense to launch in their home base. That was one of the things that worked for me. I had worked at a lot of facilities, and had done contract work through various organizations. I had a good reputation, and when I went to meet with facilities and began having these conversations, they were already familiar with me and recognized the investment I had made as a nurse. In some cases that worked to my advantage. People would say, "Do you guys remember Nicole?" which got others talking about my business as well. If you have this kind of network you should definitely be tapping into it.

On the other hand, I am not necessarily talking about your social circle. As mentioned earlier, when I started my agency I thought my nursing friends would jump on board. Instead, they were like, "Nope, can't do it." This was another tough lesson to learn (i.e. about not taking things personally), and rather than spending time being hurt and disappointed, I want you to place your focus where it should be: on building your business.

I do, however, still want you to look at your network from a strictly professional standpoint. Are you already connected with facilities? Do you have viable contacts? Understand here that you are not going to be solely relying on them. That's not the way to build your business and besides, even if everybody you know came to work for you, it would probably not be enough to meet your revenue goal. Remember, at this point you are simply mining data to determine where you should launch.

To recap, you need to be looking at vacancies, your revenue goal, and your network contacts… and the fourth factor: barriers to entry. These are the rules and regulations that differ from state to state. Some states and regions have a lower barrier of entry, meaning you can provide basic information and quickly be up and running, while others have higher barriers, meaning there are a lot of licensing requirements and bureaucracy that will make getting authorization to run a staffing firm more challenging.

Do you see why you shouldn't necessarily choose the area in which you live?

Again, everything is strategic. I'm looking at how easy or how difficult it's going to be in the market. Now, I have never seen a market that we were not able to launch in, however, but I will say that sometimes we have to modify our plan in the short run to get what we want in the long run.

It might seem counterintuitive, but sometimes it makes sense to launch in places with high barriers to entry. For example, there is one particular area where the agency owners are always going to jump through hoops but it's worth it because of the way it shapes the competitive field.

The more complex the licensing process, the more people will be filtered out, either because they don't meet the requirements or because they don't have the patience or resources to go through it. Those who do make it through will be really skilled professionals, which is also going to influence your profit…in the long run.

But what about now?

Let's say you're in an area where it's going to take five years to get licensed and up and running. I'm not saying that you shouldn't launch your staffing agency there, however, you also have to figure out how to be profitable in the interim – for example, by starting your business where there are fewer barriers to entry, while you work on the other location in the background.

As I like to say, "I want to make money while I'm waiting on it."

Again, these are lessons that I learned through my trial by fire. In the beginning, I was so determined that it didn't matter if we weren't making money. It worked out eventually, but only after I got new information and applied it during my time around.

Your geography is going to set you up for success or failure. It must also support your ultimate goals. Some of you are already running agencies and may be in a good area, but what about when it comes time for expansion?

I remember one particular coaching client. She had an amazing healthcare staffing firm, but her growth was stunted and she couldn't figure out why. Through our work together, she realized she had never considered that it might be time to strategically grow her firm in a different direction. We made a few tweaks to her base, her geography, and her model, which resulted in her agency quadrupling in size.

Regardless of the region, there is going to be a cap, which is fine as long as you can still meet your revenue goal. Let's say you have reached seven figures; you have an office with a staff of twenty andinsurance. Real things are happening! Then you realize, "Hey, there's still a demand here and I need to expand." Now you have to ask yourself whether your geography supports that expansion, meaning, is there an opportunity for you to strategically grow?

When we talk about growth, we always talk about it within the context of a specific area. What do I mean by this? I am always being asked by people to show them how to launch in New York, California, Mississippi, and so on – all at the same time. I tell them what I am going to tell you: that doesn't make sense; nor is it necessary. I explain that organic growth is the best growth, and there is a vast difference between being ambitious and forcing it.

Now, let's get into how we can figure out if there is a strategic advantage to launching in your geography of choice.

Tools of the Trade

Recall that the first thing we want to do is determine the number of vacancies in a geographical location. One inexpensive and effective tool I've found to do preliminary research is Indeed. This is a job aggregator where healthcare organizations often post jobs (though they are pulled in from other sources as well).

Let's say New York, New York is a market I'm interested in. I go on Indeed and do a search for registered nurses, where I see that there are 4,738 full-time vacancies. My assumption is that these full-time jobs are for forty hours a week.

That's 4,738 times 40, which is 189,520 hours available every week in New York for registered nurses. I'm now going to multiply that by four, meaning there are 758,080 hours available per month.

Calculating Market Share

Let's say that 1% of the facilities in New York give me a chance. That would mean I'd have 1% of the market share, or 7,580 hours per month.

Now, let's go back to our earlier example of $16 an hour as a baselineprofit margin. That means I would make $16 for every one of those 7,580 hours or $121,280 per month in profit. Multiply that by twelve and I'm making a profit of *1,455,368 per year.*

Are you shocked yet? Well, that's not all. We have not even touched the part-time or those for other job titles!

Now let's do licensed practical nurses (LPNs). Let's assume there are 1,835 full-time vacancies, again, at forty hours each week.That is 73,400 hours in New York available on a weekly basis, or 293,600 per month. With 1% of the market share, we get 2,936 hours per month for LPN coverage. Using our $16-per-hour baseline, we're going to make $46,976 on a monthly basis, or $563,172 per year. When we add this to our profit for registered nurses, we have reached two million dollars annually in profit.

When I got into the healthcare staffing industry, my mind was blown. I had no idea that this level of profitability was possible. I only teach what I know and what I've done full-time.

And we're not done yet.

Let's say there are 1,681 full-time positions for certified nursing assistants (CNAs). That brings us to 67,240 hours per week. Following the same formula, 1% of the market share would yield us over half a million dollars, which we then add to our $2 million, for a potential $2.5 million from New York alone. At this point I would go back to my revenue goal. If it's $10 million, maybe it's time to reassess. If it's $1 million, I know that New York is a good place to launch.

Brenda's Story

We had the opportunity to work with Brenda very closely. Initially she came into our self-paced program and then decided to upgrade to semi-private business development.

Brenda was facing many of the same challenges as you, but she followed this formula and, within a week of officially launching her agency, already had two contracts under review and negotiations underway with a company that had secured a government grant for a medical staffing clinic. She is a prime example of what you can accomplish when you invest in yourself and work this program.

As she said:

I am very well-prepared. I have the blueprint. I haven't had to try to recreate the wheel. It's been given to me... I'm comfortable going into rooms, talking to administrators, and picking upthe phone. I know my worth and it feels good.

After finishing this chapter, go back and look at the area you have been considering. Plug in the formula based on 1% of the market share. Please note that this is very conservative – there have been areas where I had a much larger share of the market – but you want to play it safe when calculating. If your geography doesn't support your goals at 1%, it's time to reassess your geography.

The Possibility

This chapter has given you a taste of what's possible in this field. If someone had told me this when I began this journey, I wouldn't havebelieved them. I was sitting at a desk, got fired, and decided I was going to help other nurses find jobs. Nearly two decades later, here we are.

Honestly, I didn't even want all of that backthen. I only wanted to be able to take care of my son and control my time. You have your own dreams as well – maybe they are more ambitious than mine were, maybe not. The point is that there is opportunity out there beyond your wildest imagination.

Most of us have been conditioned to know being ordinary, when we really have the innate ability to create extraordinary results. You didn't end up in this space accidentally. You ended up here for a reason. And I want you thinking about what that reason is.

Don't underestimate the work that you're doing here. You've seen how to go into these areas and do an assessment to determine if there is a viable market in your chosen area. Remember, you've got to ask the right questions to get the right answers.

Homework

Do the research on Indeed about your intended location. Is your geography viable?

_____
_____
_____
_____
_____
_____
_____
_____
_____
_____
_____
_____
_____
_____
_____
_____
_____
_____
_____
_____
_____
_____
_____
_____

What does expansion look like for you?

_____

_____

_____

_____

_____

_____

_____

_____

_____

_____

_____

_____

_____

_____

_____

_____

_____

_____

_____

_____

_____

_____

_____

_____

_____

_____

What are your ideas about abundance, or lack thereof? For example, what thoughts would be triggered if you learned that someone else was launching in the same city? Would you think, "There is enough for both of us?" or would you fall into a lack mentality and immediately start looking for another place, even though you desired location was the most viable for you?

_____
_____
_____
_____
_____
_____
_____
_____
_____
_____
_____
_____
_____
_____
_____
_____
_____
_____
_____
_____
_____
_____
_____

Chapter Three

FIND THE RICHES IN THE NICHES

*I skate to where the puck is going,
not where it has been.*

–Wayne Gretsky

I t's funny how certain conversations stick in your mind for years after you have them. I remember chatting – or more accurately, venting – to a business acquaintance. I was frustrated because we had been at six figures for a while, and I couldn't seem to move the needle.

Six figures sounds great…unless you know, as I did, that you have a seven-figure potential.

She listened without interrupting, then said matter-of-factly, "Nicole, you need help."

I always appreciate people being upfront with me, and so I'm going to be upfront with you: in my head I was replying, *No, I don't.*

In fact, I was silently continuing the whole conversation: *I'm already running a successful business; I mean, we are already at six figures. I don't have the time to watch YouTube. I'm reading books. Where do you think this is going to fit in?*

Then I stopped and thought about it, and a question popped into my head as clearly as if she had asked it: *Nicole, so if you got all the answers, why don't you have seven-figure results?*

That inner dialogue led me to invest in my first business coach. And it was no small investment, either. It was a lot of money – plus I had to travel four hours to meet this coach. I didn't know what to expect, and to be honest, I was scared about it.

The whole drive I was thinking, *Nicole, you're crazy. What are you doing? Why isn't she driving to meet you, after the investment you've made? What is this all about?*

Any doubts I had evaporated during that first session. I wasn't exactly sure how, but the coach was not only able to shift my mindset about some things, she gave me an entirely new perspective.

As we worked together, she showed me the gaps in my current strategy and helped me build the framework – one I didn't even know I needed – to support a seven-figure business.

A few months after our sessions wrapped, I was sitting in my office fighting off a sense of dread. It was that time again, time for the annual report. I remember looking at it, my dread turning to joy, and – though I knew we could do it – surprise. There were seven numbers there! How had that happened?

Though it felt like magic, it was the result of hard work, and – just as important – my realization that I didn't know what I didn't know, and I needed to leverage someone else's expertise. I can honestly say my coach is the reason I'm here today, and why my mission is to create that shift for others.

If you're reading and thinking, as I once did, "I know I can do it. I want to launch," or "I've already launched and my business is stagnant. I don't know what my next steps are, but I know I have six- or seven-figure potential," then it's time to take a look at potential gaps in your strategy, including your niche.

How Do I Validate My Niche?

What are you passionate about? Is there an area to which you feel "called?"

When figuring out your niche, these are the questions you want to start with. (By the way, this is the only time you will hear me talk about passion first. I talk about the profit first, 99.9% of the time.)

As a former nurse, I felt – and still do – feel very close to that profession. It speaks to my need to make a difference in people's lives. It's also where I had my credentials, which is not quite as important as passion, but it is a factor.

So, since I had the credentials and the passion for nursing, that's where I started my initial assessment.

Before I was a nurse I had worked as Certified Nursing Assistant (CNA), and one of the things that I hated about it was that we did all the heavy lifting. A lot of work, not a lot of reward. I promised myself that if I was ever in a position to do so, I was going to make a difference for the CNAs.

And that's exactly what I did. In fact, one of the first things I did when building my business was to really go after the CNA market. We also created some different opportunities for CNAs within our organization.

It was another passion of mine – and another area in which I had credentials.

If you're reading this and thinking, *I'm not a nurse*, bear with me. This is not a disqualifier. It is a starting place.

Once you know what your passion and your credentials are, the second thing we've got to look at is the market. I can be as passionate as I want about the CNA market, but if it doesn't exist (meaning the need doesn't exist), then it doesn't make sense to put my energy there.

How do you assess your market? Look at your revenue goal, then what vacancies exist, using the formula discussed in the previous chapter. Pull out the ones you're passionate about or feel connected to, and then make an assessment of the market using those same numbers.

Let's say, for example, you want to staff correctional facilities. Obviously, jails are not like hospitals – they are not all over the place – so you will probably have to really stretch your market (and expand your geographical area) depending on what your revenue goals are.

By the way, one of our first Launch, Growth, Thrive millionaires staffed only CNAs her first year, and generated seven-figure revenues, all because she made sure the market supported that beforehand.

Competitors

It's important to note that I very rarely talk about the competition. Why? Because I don't think competition really exists. However, I do look at other businesses in my market from the standpoint of what they are *not* doing.

For example, when I started in 2005, most of the competitors in my area did not want to touch the CNA market. They thought of it as a headache, rather than a premium market. Even for few that did staff CNAs, it wasn't a heavy focus, but an ancillary, less important position. I thought this was insane, and an untapped opportunity.

Other people in the field thought *I* was the crazy one; they thought I didn't know what I was doing. And that was how we ended up dominating the market.

It doesn't matter what anyone else thinks – if you do your market research beforehand, and follow your passion, you will be in the right place. And if you do a good job for your clients, they're going to continue to do business with you.

A lot of times your business will even expand. For example, we got into some places because we were the only ones staffing CNAs. It was the deciding factor that put us ahead of everyone else.

Passion, plus credentials, plus doing what the competition is not – that is how you carve out our niche.

Targeting a Narrow Focus

One of the things I hear most from new mentees is that there are staffing firms everywhere. Well, perhaps, but if you carve out a very specific niche, your market will not be saturated because no one can fit into it.

For example, some mentees focused on staffing professionals at dialysis clinics, which is a very specialized type of agency. Others focus solely on correctional facilities. There are staffing agencies that provide RNs and LPNs in offshore settings and staffing firms that only staff doctors' offices, or flu clinics, and so on. The narrower and more targeted you get, the more you're going to carve out a lane with a very tight fit.

This will also make marketing and naming your agency (more on that in Chapter 5) easier because potential clients with that need will know they can come to you to fill it.

Oftentimes, your focus will become even narrower with time and experience in an area. My dominant market has been long-term care facilities, staffing RNs, LPNs, and CNAs – specifically rural facilities that have experienced a turnover. Because I am in that area I know when there's been a trigger event at a facility and they're having staffing issues. That is the niche, that is how I stand out. No one wants to staff these little rural facilities because they assume a forty-bed place is not profitable, but I have made half a million in revenue from these kinds of places. Like Wayne Gretsky, I am keeping my eye on where the puck is headed.

Again, you tighten your niche by following your passion and your credentials, coupled with your due diligence to make sure there's a market left unfilled by your competitors. Remember, though, a narrow niche is not the same as narrow thinking.

I've played in the nursing space because it presented a great opportunity, but that doesn't mean you have to. You might have an agency for nurse practitioners or physician's assistants, within various aspects of healthcare. You don't have to limit it.

What Is Your Own Experience Level?

Once you select that niche, the next step is to build around it. If the market is saturated and if you show up beige, you're going to look like any other agency. Instead, figure out what sets you apart and presents a real advantage to your prospects, and you will make that niche yours.

How do you do this? By identifying your experience level. If your mind automatically starts sifting through things and saying, "I shouldn't do this" or "I don't know enough about that" – stop it! This is not about disqualifying yourself, but about determining the area(s) in which you excel. What can you offer that makes you stand out?

One of our mentees reached out to me, scared and intimidated. She said, "I just don't know what my advantage is." I reminded her of my story, which is a little like David and Goliath.

When I started out, some of my prospective clients were working with huge staffing firms that had two hundred nurses, whereas I probably didn't have twenty! I knew I couldn't compete with them on quantity, but I could compete with them on quality all day long, and that's what I focused on.

To distinguish our mentee in the marketplace, we focused on the fact that she was a new agency and didn't have a ton of clients. This means she could nurture and have more intimate relationships with the clients she did have, which put her at a competitive advantage over the larger agencies in her market.

A few months later, she called me. "The big guys are out of the building," she said, "and they've asked me to be their frontrunner." She had crossed the seven-figure mark.

What are your current "disadvantages" or things you think need to be repositioned? How can you reframe them as advantages?

For example, "No, I don't have a thousand nurses. No, I don't have a hundred, but you know what? The nurses I do have are excellent and I stand behind every nurse that works with us. I don't have the quantity, but I guarantee quality and uninterrupted operations in your facility. How does that sound?"

Healthcare Staffing Firms Under Stress

Now we're going to turn to streamlining your focus. I get calls from people who tell me about all the disciplines they staff. That's when I cut right to the chase and ask, "What's your revenue?" Oftentimes I hear that despite staffing twenty-five disciplines they are not making six figures.

This is when I tell them to streamline their focus to three disciplines or less. (I actually prefer two disciplines to start.) This will be a lot easier on your budget, and make your marketing much easier as well.

The goal is for people to talk about what you do. You want organic word of mouth to create an ebb and flow and organic traffic for your business. If you just have a few therapists talking about you over here, a few therapists over here, a few nurses over here, it's not really building the traction you need. However, when you streamline, when you zoom in on a couple of areas, you generate more buzz. All of a sudden you're not having to work as hard on marketing, because more people in your marketing are talking about you, which leads to referrals.

When your focus is streamlined, prospective clients are able to find t*hemselves* more easily. If I had a web page that read, "I'm going to teach you how to start a healthcare staffing firm and run an online business... And I'm going to teach you how to start a commercial cleaning business. I'll teach you how to run it and about direct selling..." (all of which I know how to do) you'll get lost in that messaging. But because we specifically talked about you – the healthcare staffing firm owner or aspiring healthcare staffing firm owner – you buy it. You need to create that in your own agency as well.

Savannah's Journey

I met Savannah when she participated in one of our challenges. A former travel nurse, she had been wanting to start her own staffing firm for about a year but wasn't sure how to go about it; she didn't know how to make the pieces fit and like I had all those years ago, she realized she needed help. She made a commitment at that time and continued working with me and our team.

We gave her the tools to identify her passion and her credentials, and used them to carve out a niche.

I always say it's not just about information, but revelation. Everybody has information, but until you understand why it works, you can't put it into action. This is why I teach the way I teach. If I just told you to do something and you did it, that's the farthest you're going to go. But if I tell you *why* I did it, then when you have the context and the reasoning behind it to help you understand the process behind those important decisions. You have the power and the control over your business.

I knew Savannah really got it when I read her testimonial:

Through this program, I've grown not only into a business owner, *I've grown as a person.* Nicole doesn't just offer the training you need to jump in and gain business sense – she also *speaks volumes in life.*

This is the secret sauce, and what I am most trying to convey: the skills and the mindset you need to succeed in your business are the same ones you need to live an empowered life overall. They go hand in hand.

Like so many others, Savannah's biggest mindset shift was in understanding true confidence comes from within and that going from nurse to business owner was an attainable dream.

"I don't have to reach for the stars anymore," she said, "That the star is here."

Again, belief in yourself is the key; it will take you through the inevitable days when running a business feels like one challenge after another. It doesn't matter if you are walking into a facility or making a phone call or negotiating a contract – you show up *knowing* you are holding a powerful solution in your hand and that *you belong there.*

Help to Launch, Grow, Thrive

As mentioned, Savannah joined a challenge then signed up to be a part of our private development community. There, we go through each step that I am talking about here in greater detail, from the introduction to the healthcare staffing industry to principals for growth and tools to determine your state requirements and ensure you're compliant. We also have a library full of contracts, forms, and resources that my team has put together so you don't have to reinvent the wheel.

I share how I worked on my business for years without a grant or a loan, as well as how to find the right clients and the right candidates. Remembering that not everyone is your ideal client or candidate will help you stay focused on the people and things that will get you where you need to go – and on that narrow niche you've carved out for yourself.

We talk about how to avoid the pitfalls that can lead to failure.

The number one thing I see with healthcare staffing firm owners is that they're undereducated. They think that because they have a contract and nurses, they have a business when the truth is that is only part of it.

Then there is the community aspect, which is invaluable for two reasons: one, you have people to celebrate your wins, something far too many of us don't have. This is a very important point that I need to expand upon – it's what I call "friend power."

In work and in life, as you start reaching new levels you will require new things and you will need to find new friends. I have two friends I've known for twenty years; the rest are relationships I have cultivated along my journey. Don't wait for the right people to show up. Work on becoming the person you want to attract, and the right friends, coaches, and partners from all races and walks of life will show up. Some people may look like you and some may not, but they will be there to help. *They will be helping to serve your mission.*

Second, and related to that point, is the accountability you will find in the community, both from fellow members and the amazing group of coaches who walk the program alongside you as you do the work, identify your needs, and create a framework based on your geography and revenue goals. In fact, the niche I have been discussing in this chapter should actually be the driver for your revenue goal.

To illustrate this, let's return for a moment to the New York City example from the previous chapter. If you were staffing RNs, LPNs, and CNAs, you could easily reach a million-dollar revenue goal. And let's say your forerunner was registered nurses, so that is where the heavy weight would be. Now, look at your offers and see if there is a narrower niche you can carve out within your market that can drive real revenue.

Everything else should be supplemental to whatever you choose as your forerunner. Now, do you have enough business to support it in that geography? Remember, I try to keep it to two for our purposes here let's choose one to focus on. If you don't have business for it, go to the next niche, always keeping in mind to focus on what has the greatest opportunity.

If you find your current niche does not support your revenue goals, you have a decision to make. For example, if you're trying to work with correctional facilities and you say, "Wait, now I've identified my means but this work doesn't exist in my geography," you can either modify your niche (i.e. to dialysis techs, medical coders, etc.) or expand your geographical region.

Finally, always keep your eyes on where the puck is going. People thought I was crazy when I started my business during the time of Hurricane Katrina, but it turned out my first employees were from New Orleans and so were my first nurses. Today, with the global pandemic and subsequent events like the Great Resignation, the world is transitioning on an even greater scale and more rapidly than at any other time in recent history. As a result, there are new and incredible opportunities – or "riches in the niches." Your job is to open your mind and do the work in order to find them. Remember, while working on your business is difficult, being an employee is too, so when challenges arise, "choose your hard" and keep moving.

Homework

What is your niche and how will it help you tap into the potential for profitability?

_____

_____

_____

_____

_____

_____

_____

_____

_____

_____

_____

_____

_____

_____

_____

_____

_____

_____

_____

_____

_____

_____

_____

_____

_____

_____

Take a look at your current relationships. Are you surrounding yourself with like-minded people (those who are constantly growing and elevating) or those who are helping you maintain your status quo?

_____

_____

_____

_____

_____

_____

_____

_____

_____

_____

_____

_____

_____

_____

_____

_____

_____

_____

_____

_____

_____

_____

_____

_____

What is your belief system around relationships and the willingness of others to offer support and guidance? You might spend some time journaling about some things that may have shaped these beliefs (i.e. things you witnessed, heard, or experienced). Are they empowering you, or holding you back? If it's the latter, it's time to let them go.

_____

_____

_____

_____

_____

_____

_____

_____

_____

_____

_____

_____

_____

_____

_____

_____

_____

_____

_____

_____

_____

_____

_____

_____

_____

Chapter Four

COLLAPSE THE TIME CODE

Your greatest asset is your earning ability.
Your greatest resource is your time.

—Brian Tracy

So far we've discussed some of the tools and logistics you need to set your revenue goals, identify your geography, and carve out a "tight lane," or niche, for your health-care staffing business. Now we're going to expand that conversation a bit to something just as important to your success: collapsing the time code. If you're thinking that sounds like something out of a fantastical science fiction movie, think again. It's actually an achievable – and critical – piece of building, not only a successful company, but a successful life.

Remember in the previous chapter I talked about stepping into the person you were meant to become? Well, that person understands that profit is not just about revenue, but about the freedom and the ability to balance the personal and the professional. For me, it was the ability to take two years off to be a wife and a mother and still be making money. It was also figuring out how to go from being a forty-hour-a-week CEO to achieving the same things in twenty hours.

Jim Rohn said, "Time is our most valuable asset, yet we tend to waste it, kill it and spend it rather than invest it." I like to say, "Money didn't bring me happiness; happiness brought me money" – and part of that process was learning how to harness my time and use it efficiently.

I can remember when I was first thinking about starting a business. There was so much to do to get there, and the dream seemed really distant. So what did I do? I made it even more so, by hiding.

Your business will rise and fall per the level of knowledge you have. *You get what you believe.* Maybe your life is good, but there's always another level, and to reach it you must be willing to grow and evolve. If nothing changes, nothing changes.

How did I hide back then? Well, I hid behind "letters" by getting more education. I hid behind promotions as I climbed the administrative ladder in nursing. I started hiding behind increased salaries, too, yet that dream of having my own business just wouldn't go away.

Then, one day, I gave myself permission to identify with that feeling. I had to align myself to the fact that I had been chosen for something different and that nursing was not my destination, but an avenue I would pass through on the way to get there.

This in no way diminishes the enormous respect and gratitude for the nursing profession and all who serve in it. I have loved ones and friends who are nurses and I am in awe of the work they do. We all should be in awe of the nurses that saw us through the worst of the pandemic, at great personal risk, and showed the world once and for all that they truly are the backbone of the healthcare industry.

Here's what I had to work out: I can respect and honor those who are chosen to be at patients' bedsides, and do the heavy lifting each day – and acknowledge some of us who are chosen for something different. I was one of the people, and the fact that you're reading this makes me believe that you're one of them too.

Maybe you have been feeling this too, that no matter how many degrees and certifications you earn and how many promotions you get, you have that sense that won't go away, there is something more out there for you. If so, you will have to, as I did, give yourself permission to take ownership of it. For it is that feeling that will propel you to success.

Tony Robbins has said, "Success leaves clues." I believe that it's true, and I also firmly believe that *sustainable* success leaves an entire blueprint. You have to follow that blueprint by doing specific things to create specific results.

Let's Talk Time

It would have been the easiest thing in the world for me, after being fired and escorted from the building that day, to get another nursing job. I had a great reputation; I had the accolades. I could have continued along the same path and gone miles up the road. The biggest thing that stopped me – and made me decide to step out of my comfort zone – was time.

More than anything, I wanted to own my time. Remember, I was just twenty-six years old, had already achieved a level of success, and was on my way to more. Yet I knew that if I simply moved into another nursing job, I would never have what was most important to me.

Today, I live my life according to Proverbs 9:11: "Wisdom will make the hours of your day more profitable and the years of your life more fruitful." Back then, when I read it, I thought, *Oh, that sounds great. But what does it mean?*

I started dissecting it and really thinking about how I could apply it to my life. Wisdom is the quality of having experience, having knowledge, and having good judgment – in other words, the quality of being wise. How then, did wisdom correlate to generating more profit? And what was profit, anyway?

Profit is a financial game. It can be something that's more beneficial to my life. As for "fruitful," most people associate it with having children; however, the larger meaning is about producing results, producing a good outcome.

So, if wisdom was going to make the hours of my day more profitable and the years of my life, more fruitful, that meant there had to be a better way to do what I was doing. That's when I started thinking about where I could find the expertise I needed, and what profit looked like in my life.

Ask yourself that right now: what does it look like in your life? Notice I didn't say *in your bank account,* but in your *life.* Most people think because I talk about revenue a lot that this is my definition of profit – and yes, to an extent that's true – but there is much more to it than that. Profit is the ability, I mentioned earlier, to take two years off from my organization and spend time with my husband and children when they needed me, to never have to ship my kids off on the school bus or to daycare or a babysitter's. It was being able to sit at the bedside of a loved one while they were transitioning – all without missing a beat in terms of revenue. There is no job that would have given me that opportunity, so that was not only profitable, it was like striking gold.

Again, what does profit look like for you? More vacations? More time with the people you love, be it a partner, kids, relatives, and friends? It is being able to create more income as you do this? Is it about just having more options in life?

Next, let's look at what it means to be fruitful. I remember being so excited as I looked over the numbers with one of my previous mentors.

I also remember when she turned to me and said, "Nicole, I don't want to offend you, but you are a big fish in a small pond."

I wasn't angry, but I do remember thinking, *Did I just pay this woman to tell me off? Really?*

She left it there, but the next time we spoke, she said, "I know you're excited about your results, but I'm not impressed."

She then asked me who I was impacting. "You're generating profit, yes, but you're also hiding in your office. You have something other people can learn from. You can teach other people how to do this. So, no, I'm not impressed with your numbers."

(By the way, this lady had generated $103 million in revenue at that time, so it's safe to say she knew what she was talking about.)

My numbers, though in the seven figures, were substantially lower, but that was beside the point. What she was really saying was that my present way of doing things was not fruitful. Showing others how to do what I was doing would *change lives*. Talk about a day of reckoning – and a huge wake-up call about what was really possible for me.

To be honest, I didn't want to do what she was suggesting. I was like, "I'm good. I'm in my office. I'm making money. Nobody knows me.

My doors close. I run in, run out. Life is good."

Then I had this dream...

It was about something that happened at an airport, but the significance was what it symbolized for me. It was as if God was saying, "Yes, you paid a price, but these people cannot take off unless you get on the plane." After I tried to dismiss my mentor's advice, He showed up and delivered the same message in a different way. That dream changed my mind, and here we are.

Who is waiting on you to produce fruit? What opportunities are you supposed to be creating in your healthcare staffing firm right now? What facilities are waiting for your staff because they need that stability to run successfully? Whose loved one, what resident, what patient, is only going to get the proper care if their facility is adequately staffed?

Do you see the shift in thinking those questions create? It is the same shift my mentor – and the dream – created for me. It reminded me that I was chosen for something different, something bigger – even bigger than generating revenue. That shift was the beginning of me always asking myself, "Okay, what's next?"

What's next for you? Whatever it is, there must be fruit from it. If you're saying you want more time, you want more income, you want more freedom, I believe that wisdom is the path. I believe wisdom is the *only* path.

Though I didn't fully appreciate it at the time (seriously, I was giving her the side eyes) that mentor, with her simple words, changed my life. I know she truly was not trying to offend me, she was saying:

"Girl, you're not doing nothing. I'm not saying that to demean you. I am saying that because I see the things in you that you don't see in yourself."

Types of Healthcare Staffing Firms

Typically, there are four ways to go if you want to run a healthcare staffing firm. There is the franchise model, where you work with an established agency and buy access to their branding. (The cost typically ranges from $40-$50,000 to a couple of hundred thousand.) While this has benefits and is a form of ownership, there are limitations on being able to create your own processes and systems and things like that, because they retain co-ownership.

Then there is the consulting option, of which I am *not* a huge advocate. In this scenario, someone with business expertise assists you in setting up your company. The issue is that they may lack specific knowledge of the healthcare staffing industry and therefore will not be able to properly advise you on the various ins and outs, including potential pitfalls.

I hear from many people who have engaged consultants. They tell me, "I got my LLC, I got my EIN. I'm set up, but now I don't know how to run this." By this point they have already made a large investment – sometimes to the tune of $15,000 to $30,000 for a couple of weeks (or even days) of consulting – and at the end of it, they are left with a very fragmented solution.

Then there's the DIY (Do-It-Yourself) option. This is where you put the pieces together and figure things out on your own – kind of like when you follow the YouTube video on how to add an accent wall or update your kitchen cabinets. And just like those projects, the DIY approach to your business typically doesn't have the same initial investment as franchising or consulting but is often the option that winds up costing the most.

As mentioned earlier, I learned this lesson the hard way. When I started, I had a DIY mentality, thinking, "I'm gonna figure this out, and it will be fine." That's what I did, and for a while it was. That first year my business was profitable, and it was the year after that as well. Then came 2007, when I lost everything, spent nine months licking my wounds, and had to start all over.

This was a huge price to pay – not only financially, but emotionally. If only I had listened when people told me, "Hey, you need a coach. You need to invest. You need to connect with someone who's done this before," I would have saved myself a lot of money, a lot of heartache and, most importantly, a lot of time.

This is the biggest reason I believe the DIY option is the one that sets you up for the most failure: a lack of accountability I mentioned in the previous chapter. Without the support and guidance of someone with expertise, when faced with challenges we might be tempted to say, "It's just not working" and throw up our hands.

That's the place where dreams don't get built. This is why you need someone, not to do it for you, but to do it with you.

Thanks to that mentor, walking others through this process is my life's work and my legacy. That said, I only work with those who are willing to do the inner and outer work, who are willing to show up for themselves in a challenge every day.

Here is a story that illustrates what I am talking about. When I started this journey nearly two decades ago, I had a friend by my side. She was every bit as excited as I was about launching a healthcare staffing firm. We talked about it and rooted for each other constantly… for a month or two. Then her excitement started dwindling.

Fast forward to today. She is working as a nurse, which is amazing unless you have been chosen for something else, which I believe she was. I often think about what would have happened for her if she just would have continued the journey. But we all have free will, and at some point, she decided it was better to just suppress the desire and do what was necessary to move forward.

I also think about what my life would be like today if I had gone back to nursing instead of starting my staffing firm. I got my answer the year my husband came to me, our tax returns in hand.

"Nicole," he aside, "What would you be making now if you had stayed in the same nursing position?"

I told him I would probably be at about $60,000 a year, and doing a lot of work for it. I would have missed a lot of my kids' games, and I'd probably be burnt out.

As he handed me our tax return, he said, "Nicole, this year, you earned $1.925 million..."

We divided that by 60,000 and realized I had bought *thirty years* of my time. That's how long it would have taken me to reach that amount working as a nurse. Instead, because of one decision to say, "No, I'm going forward. I'm going to step out in faith and do what I believe I am being called to do," my life, along with hundreds of healthcare staffing firm owners, was drastically changed for the better.

I'm sharing this so you can see yourself in the journey. What is that one decision for you? How would making it change your life, and impact the lives of others? If you were able to collapse time, how would you be able to show up? Who would you be able to show up for?

I hope the first person is yourself.

Homework

What is your why? (What is profitable for you outside this journey?)

_____

_____

_____

_____

_____

_____

_____

_____

_____

_____

_____

_____

_____

_____

_____

_____

_____

_____

_____

_____

_____

_____

_____

_____

_____

_____

What is your definition of fruitful, i.e., how many jobs can you create? How many facilities can you help? This is not just about service to self. Yes, at first it is, but then it begins to produce fruit – for example, the advice of my mentor led me to uplevel my life, which in turn led to helping others change theirs. What ripple effect do you want to create?

_____

_____

_____

_____

_____

_____

_____

_____

_____

_____

_____

_____

_____

_____

_____

_____

_____

_____

_____

_____

Chapter Five

NAMING YOUR STAFFING AGENCY

One day, many years ago, my husband Dwayne found me sitting in my closet crying because I had (in my mind) quit my business again. And I wasn't just crying – I was pulling clothes down, I was throwing shoes around. I mean, this was high drama, a full-blown pity party.

When Dwayne asked what I was doing, I sobbed, "I just don't care anymore," then waited for him to come and embrace me. Instead, he said, "Stop that. Stop. That there's nothing emotional about business. Cry later. Make decisions, get a strategy. Quit being so emotional."

Dwayne is my partner, my best friend, and my dearest love. What he is not is someone who is going to yes me to death or coddle me when I am not operating as my best self.

That day, he gave me the best advice of my life. He encouraged me to cultivate what I needed most at that point: emotional maturity. Some of the challenges I was facing I had brought on myself, due in part to a lack of that maturity. He taught me, for example, to go into meetings without my identity wrapped up in the outcome.

How does this relate to the naming of your agency? Well, because for many people their identity is wrapped up in the name, which is blinding them to certain realities – for example, the huge role a name plays in your agency's success. I know this because I see a lot of agency names out there and am often left wondering what they mean. And if I am left to wonder, it means you are not drawing the attention of the right prospective clients and candidates.

To illustrate this, I'll share the story behind the name of my agency: Quality Medical Staffing.

I remember healthcare professionals coming into our building – and often interrupting our normal processes. While I was excited and grateful for the help and the support that they were bringing into our healthcare organizations, I also remember thinking, *We have a lot of people, but we just really need quality people. We need people that are going to come in, understand, and be an asset to our process, rather than interrupting it.*

When I began preparing my agency, I had no idea what I was going to call it. I was brainstorming, putting all these ideas together and jotting them down. Then one day, while driving down a busy freeway in my area, I saw a sign that read "QMS." It stood for Quality Machine Services.

"Oh, I love it!" I exclaimed. I loved the simplicity. I loved the logo. Most of all, I loved that I knew exactly what they provided.

I was still thinking about it when I got home later that day, and it just resonated. "Quality," I said, "That's what I've been saying! I want to build quality medical staffing... Q M S."

I would like to tell you that there was some deeper thought process to how I came up with the name, but there really wasn't. Remember, we're not trying to overcomplicate this or reinvent the wheel.

I saw something and was able to make it my own because it really expressed and brought meaning to my agency.

Now, let's dissect the reasons that name worked.

One of the reasons we were so successful with that name is that our clients could clearly identify who we were and what our brand was about. When I started approaching facilities and said, "Quality Medical Staffing," they didn't have to do any guesswork. They instantly knew what we were providing.

I've seen names like "ABC Medical Services." Unless they have a very well-crafted tagline or some other explanation, I would have no idea what that means. This is precisely what you want to avoid. You want your name to be recognizable the second someone says it or hears it.

Now, think about my program, Launch Your Healthcare Staffing Firm: Launch, Grow and Thrive in the Healthcare Staffing Industry. It's very clear what we are offering, whereas, if I just said, Launch, Grow, Thrive, that could mean a million things. It would throw off our potential clients and our prospects, and lead to countless missed opportunities.

When you're thinking of your name, you want it to be something that's easy to say; you want it to be something that's brandable.

> **Note: *brandable* is not the same thing as *personal*.**

If I named my staffing firm after myself and all of my kids, that might be meaningful to me, but not necessarily meaningful – or marketable – to my potential clients. Brandable means it's clear and succinct to everyone in your market, and those tangential to that market.

You want something that you can grow with, for example, if you decide to franchise and/or expand to other states. No one will want to step into a brand or agency that the market will not recognize.

This brings us back to the emotional maturity I mentioned earlier. Don't be so personally connected to your name that it becomes a limitation you will have to overcome later. It needs to be easy to say, easy to remember, and, again, have a meaning that is easily discernable by others. If you have a name with meaning, have an entire marketing message.

Quality Medical Staffing instantly had meaning for me. I didn't have a huge quantity of nurses, so that wasn't going to be what I was offering. What I didn't have was a pool of quality nurses, and that became my platform and my message. Over time, that name evolved from a message to a movement. That's the kind of growth I am talking about.

Think about why you even want to start your healthcare staffing firm. What's the driving force? Then look for the words that would express those ideals and concepts to others.

Other names – including those of some of our mentees – have stood out to me as excellent examples. One of them was Aligned Medical Staff and it stood out to me not just because the name was catchy, but because of the message she attached to it.

That message was, "There has to be an alignment." This name wasn't about her, but creating a marketable message and a brand she could grow with. I could immediately see her going in so many different directions, and it all started with choosing the right name.

You want something that people in the healthcare space are going to notice and remember. My agency used to be located near a medical plaza at a really busy intersection, and I had a huge sign outside that only cost around three hundred dollars but was worth its weight in gold.

Doctors and nurses would pass by that complex on their way to lunch, and then my phone would ring. "Hey," they'd say, "I've been passing here for a couple of weeks and I noticed your name, Quality Medical Staffing. Do you staff clinics? Do you staff hospitals? Do you staff assisted living communities?"

Why were they able to connect? Because it clearly communicated what we did. Now, it could have said Quality Healthcare Staffing or Quality Nurse Staffing – you get my point – because they have the same simplicity and clarity.

A lot of individuals tell me things like, "I don't want to box myself in. I want to end up doing other types of staffing." That's fine, but my advice is to cross that road when you get there. Start by going narrow so you can make it easy on yourself, and easy on your clients to find you. **MAKING LIFE EASY OR HARD**

I want to say something now about easy and hard. I used to go to work every day, punch a time clock, trade dollars for hours, have to get permission to take vacations, work extra shifts to get the things that we wanted and the lifestyle that we wanted. That was much harder than what I do now, *much* harder.

Now, what I am valued for is being able to create solutions for others. That is what you will be able to do when you start your healthcare staffing firm and help ensure that people will get the best possible care.

We've been sold on the idea that it has to be hard, that it has to be the grind, the hustle, which to some means giving up the bulk of their precious time. "You've got to put in your eighty hours," they say. But that's really not true. I know, because I've lived both ways.

Now I'm paid to think and create solutions. I want you to understand that I'm not saying that one is necessarily better than the other. I'm trying to introduce you to a new perspective because sometimes we make things hard that don't have to be hard, because we're so used to hard. I do what I do so you don't have to take years or decades saying, "What do I do now? What should I do next? Did I do this right? How do I do this? Why haven't I done that?"

Remember, you get to choose your hard, and things like naming your business don't have to be.

Homework

Brainstorm around a name that is congruent with your messaging, now and in the future.

_____

_____

_____

_____

_____

_____

_____

_____

_____

_____

_____

_____

_____

_____

_____

_____

_____

_____

_____

_____

_____

_____

_____

_____

After going through the steps in the book, think again about your identity. How is that separate from the brand you are creating for your business?

_____

_____

_____

_____

_____

_____

_____

_____

_____

_____

_____

_____

_____

_____

_____

_____

_____

_____

_____

_____

_____

_____

_____

_____

What is staying the same already costing you?

_____

_____

_____

_____

_____

_____

_____

_____

_____

_____

_____

_____

_____

_____

_____

_____

_____

_____

_____

_____

_____

_____

_____

_____

_____

_____

_____

_____

In Conclusion

Thank you for joining me on this journey. It has been an honor and a pleasure to share with you my formula for success in the healthcare staffing industry. To wrap this book up, I'm going to share a personal story that illustrates everything I've told you about emotional maturity, and about accepting guidance and help when you need it.

Back in 2005, my new staffing firm was doing very well. I was super excited every day because my dream had become a reality. Then, a couple of weeks in, I got a call from a client telling me they can't pay the invoice on time. In fact, he didn't know when he was going to be able to pay.

I sat there in complete and utter shock. I had been so happy, just to be open, to have an office, to contracts with clients and nurses working. I thought you send people a bill and they're going to pay the bill on time and then you pay the nurses. Well, that's not what happened, and we were now two days away from payroll with no way to meet it.

I remember telling a friend, "Oh my God, I won't be able to pay the nurses!" It was $2,000, which, looking back, is not a lot compared to payrolls that have come after. But in that moment it might as well have been ten times as much.

"Nicole,' my friend said, "I've known you for a long time. We went to nursing school together. I know that you are a woman of integrity. We're going to get on this phone and we're going to call these nurses and let them know."

I wanted to say, *Why in the world would we do that? Can't we just pack up and go?* But I agreed. And then, like some cosmic joke, the makeshift desk I had been using fell apart, I mean, literally collapsed to the floor, taking the computer with it. Now I was on the verge of tears because that's what was happening to my dream; it was falling apart right in front of my eyes.

Then my phone began to ring...

If was a friend I had talked to about business off and on. We had lost contact recently, and now there he was, asking, "Hey, did you ever start that business?"

"Yeah, I did, but I'm probably about to close because I owe people money."

When people work, they want to get paid. I know I do, so I could totally understand how these nurses would feel when I told them what was happening. In my head, I saw them burning the whole building down.

I told him that and he said, "Can I take you to lunch?"

Now, I'm thinking, "*This dude has more nerves than he has sense,*" but when I told my other friend in the office, she said,

"Go, go, go, we'll make the phone calls when you come back, just get out of the office."

And so I went with him, still mentally preparing myself to break the news to the nurses, and was shocked when he asked me where I bank. I told him, and he asked how much I needed. I told him that too, and he said, "Let's go to your bank."

Instead of lunch, he made an investment in my business. I was able to make payroll and the nurses never knew any different.

When I got back to the office, my desk was standing up again. My other friend had picked up the desk, chair, and computer, and fixed it all up so it looked like something semi-normal. I told her that he had given me the money and she said, "I knew it was all gonna work out. I was praying when you were gone. I knew it was going to work out one way or the other."

That man was Dwayne, and a few months later he became my husband.

As beautiful as this story is, I want you to know that that's the scary way to do business. Dwayne challenged me and taught me many of the lessons that I've shared in this book. And I was not always easy to teach. He would say things like, "I don't know what you're doing, but some of this… I think you need help." And I was telling him, "No, I've got this. And what makes you think you know about this business, anyway? You're in a completely different industry."

What I eventually came to understand was that I knew a lot about staffing and about nursing, and I knew a lot about loving people, but I didn't know much about business, and definitely not as much as Dwayne did.

He taught me honor. He taught me what it looks like to really love people, and he taught me how to stand up and be a real CEO, not just a nurse that has some shindigs, some gigs, and some business.

Since then we've walked side by side, building our healthcare staffing firm, taking it national within thirty-six months of starting, creating thousands of jobs, creating thousands of solutions, generating millions in revenue, and now sitting here and preparing other entrepreneurs to do the same thing.

I am not a god. I'm not a guru. What I am is very grateful to God for all the blessings life has brought me, and yet I know that it is bigger than me. This organization and mission have become so much bigger than me. One of the things I believe is that He has blessed me because He knew I would share those blessings with others. That is my only intention – to share information so you don't have to do the hard work that I had to do. It was worth it, but it was hard and it doesn't have to be.

And I write these words, I don't want to speak to your mind. I don't want to speak to your logic. I don't want to speak to your philosophy. I don't want to speak to your theology. I want to speak to your spirit – the part of you that knows you belong. The part of you that knows that you're playing it small right now, the part of you that knows you've been hiding.

Sometimes we're so wired to think and do a certain thing that we've got to fight ourselves before we can even begin to build something. I can't speak to why people fail because I don't necessarily know…there are so many variables. What I can tell you is why people succeed. People succeed because they get information and they commit to the process.

They stop waiting for somebody else to say, "Hey, it's right for you to go out there and be great. It's right for you to go out there and change the world. It's right for you to go out there and create amazing solutions. They stop waiting for somebody to say that and they understand the truth, that they need to be the person to say, "Yeah, it is right. And I'm ready."

Ready to Take the Next Step?

If you're ready to create a massive income and make an incredible impact in the healthcare staffing industry, I'm calling you higher. This is your sign to step into your purpose and learn how to cultivate the life you deserve.

Visit **www.launchmystaffingfirmnow.com** to take the next step today.

Bonus Gift

Scan the QR Code below for access to our exclusive Success Story vault! Don't just let this book do the talking, listen to some of our most transformational testimonies told first-hand by our program graduates.

About the Author

When it comes to helping nurses and other highly motivated professionals launch their own staffing firms, no one does it better than Nicole R. Caillier, Ph.D. Known as "The Queen of Staffing," Nicole has made it her mission to provide aspiring, emerging, and established entrepreneurs with the exact blueprint and strategies she used to build her own staffing empire, Quality Staffing Network, LLC. She has helped countless clients create unbelievable success, financial freedom, and career satisfaction by entering the healthcare staffing industry. In the past four years alone, she has established over four hundred healthcare staffing firms.

Nicole's entrepreneurial journey sprung from a desire to make a difference in the healthcare community on a greater scale in the aftermath of Hurricane Katrina. After losing her job as a nurse, she started her healthcare staffing firm in 2005 and tripled the business within two years – in the middle of a recession. Named as one of the top female business leaders in North America, Nicole has been recognized for her work by *Women in Business, Entrepreneur magazine, Charisma Magazine,* and the Impact Network. In a career full of huge wins, she's most proud of obtaining an honorary doctorate and building two multimillion-dollar businesses without additional loans or grants. An in-demand speaker, Nicole is well-versed in several topics including staffing, finding one's purpose, and building a seven-figure business. Nicole can teach your audience to reclaim their time, earn unlimited income and create the freedom they've always wanted, and tap into their true potential.